THAT'S NOT OKAY! ©
A BOOK TEACHING CHILDREN ASSERTIVENESS AND APPROPRIATE BOUNDARIES
BY: Essence Cohen Fields, LPC

## Dedication

To Ansel and our Acey Doo, thank you for your unwavering love, support, and laughter. For bringing out the best in me, always.

This book was written so that children-our most valuable yet vulnerable and precious population- can advocate for themselves and feel empowered with the help of family and friends.

First Printing, 2021

ISBN 978-1-7362235-0-5 (Printed)

ISBN 978-1-7362235-1-2 (Digital)

www.FLYCounseling.com

We all come from different families, cultures, and backgrounds
but no matter what, it is very clear that we are all loved!
The people in our lives love us so much, that they get so excited
and can't wait to show us off!
They introduce us to so many others-
friends, dads, neighbors, teachers, cousins, sisters,
mothers, and brothers!

These people may want to show us how much they love and care for us,
and sometimes they may do this with the way they touch.
They show us their love by giving us hugs and kisses, hive-fives and tickles,
our favorite games, food and even the giggles!
Most of the time this is fun and great,
but if we feel uncomfortable we have to let them know
"that's not okay!"

"That's Not Okay!"

Bodies: The people in our lives who love us make it very clear,
which parts of our bodies are not to be shared.
Although it is our job to always wash and stay clean,
there are parts of our bodies that should not be seen.
And even though the people in our lives may like to hug
and give us love,
there are still parts of our bodies that should not be touched.

If these private parts of our bodies have been touched, seen, or shared
it is important that we tell someone that we trust and love because they will care.
It is also important to know that these parts of our bodies are not to be shown.
If anyone tries to make us we have to let someone we love and trust know.
So if anyone tries to make you show your body parts to them in any way,
you must tell them, "Stop, no way! That's NOT OKAY!"

List some people in your life that you love and trust

_____

_____

_____

Secrets:

Secrets are things people tell us to keep, private and quiet, and to not share a peep!
This is good, but only for certain things.
If ever someone does something bad to you and asks you to keep it a secret,
this is when you must be sure tell and not try to keep it.


*Families to child*- Why do you think someone may ask you to keep a secret?
Discuss the difference between a good secret and a bad secret;
i.e. a surprise party vs. inappropriate touching.

Telling someone:
When you are away from your
family and loved ones for a while,
be sure to tell them everything that happened
because they love you and you are their child.
Whether you were at school, at camp,
with the babysitter, or just next door,
share all of the who, what,
when, where, whys, hows and more.

Tell your grandma, grandpa, aunt, uncle, mom, or dad-
about everything that you did, and
all about the time you had.
Be sure to share the good and the bad
because the people who love you will not be mad.
Tell them if anyone made you feel happy, excited, glad,
or even if someone said something really funny
that made you laugh!
And remember, it is even more important
to tell your loved ones if anyone
made you feel afraid, angry, or sad.

**Has anyone ever made you feel this way?**

If ever you are away from your loved
ones and someone said or did something
to make you feel embarrassed or scared,
your loved ones will want to know so you
must share.
When people try to hurt us
or make us do something that we don't
want to do in any way,
it is important that we yell as loud as we can,

**"THAT'S NOT OKAY!"**

Shame, blame: When bad things happen to us we can feel ashamed. That means we may feel embarrassed and don't know who to blame. Not telling anyone, and putting blame on ourselves is not helpful, it will only make us feel more sad and shameful

Being able to recognize who in our lives we can trust will make it easier to share our love.

Worth/Value:

You should know and understand
that you are special and important
all the way from your toes to your hand!
From your head, to your feet, and everything in between
you mean so much to so many people,
and if you ask them they all would agree!
Which is why if anyone says or does something harmful
you must remember that you will always be valuable,
unique, and exceptional!

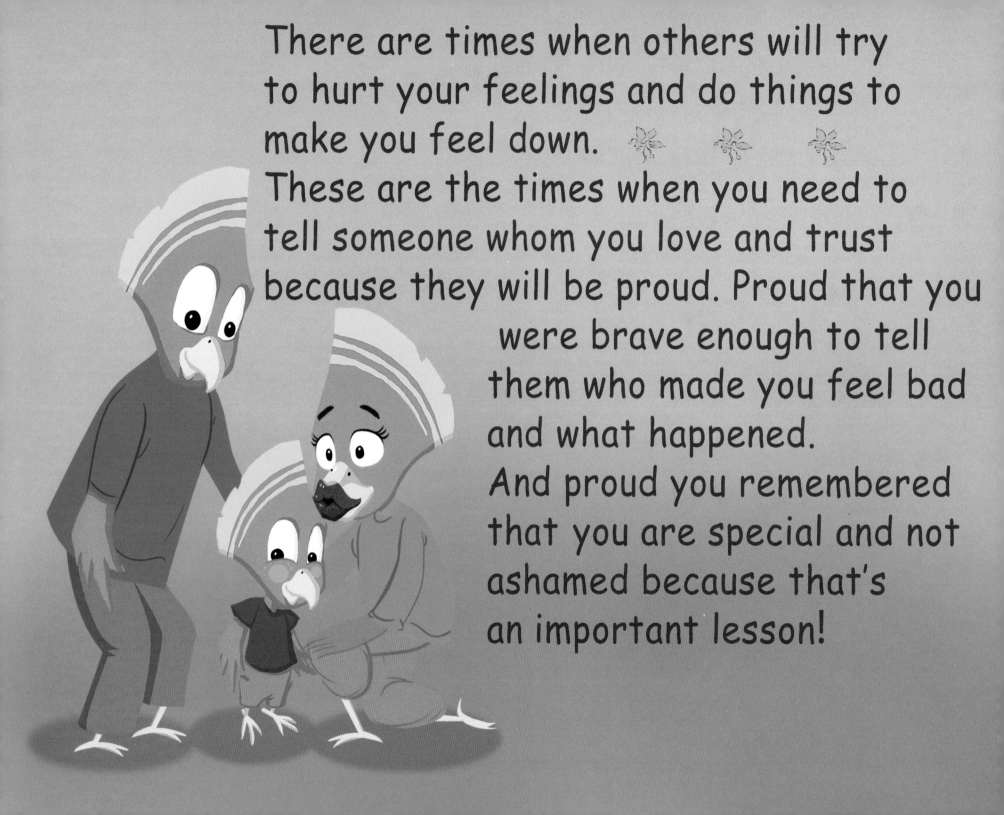

There are times when others will try to hurt your feelings and do things to make you feel down.
These are the times when you need to tell someone whom you love and trust because they will be proud. Proud that you were brave enough to tell them who made you feel bad and what happened.
And proud you remembered that you are special and not ashamed because that's an important lesson!

Say this loud everyday,
I am special and loved in every way.
And if anyone tries to touch me in a harmful way,
I will shout to them and say,

**'THAT'S NOT OKAY!'**

**Note to parents and families:**

Children often like to engage in imaginary play which at times may involve some form of physical contact. For example, playing "house" or "doctor" are imaginative play games that may involve or evolve into touch. Instead you can suggest to your child that he or she play "school", "grocery-store shopping" or even a talent show to foster their healthy creativity. These games are less likely to involve or evolve into physical contact-unless your child is possibly reenacting something they saw or experienced. In this case, you will want to further explore this with them through supportive and non-judgmental questions about an experience they may have had or witnessed.

## Exploratory Conversation Considerations:

*Use supportive reminder statements:* 'We love you no matter what', 'We can get through this', 'You're still a good boy/girl even if a bad thing happened'.

*Non-Judgmental Questions:* 'Has anyone ever told you to keep a secret that you didn't want to keep?', 'Has anyone made you feel afraid to be around them?', 'Is there anything you wish you could tell me but feel embarrassed or ashamed about?', 'Have you ever had a situation where you wanted to tell someone 'That's Not Okay!'?"

*Remember:* When a child discloses to an adult, the adult's reaction will affect the child's recovery. Remain calm, remain supportive, remain inquisitive. Thank you for creating a safe space in your child's life!

In the event there is a disclosure of abuse please call the National Child Abuse Hotline: 1.800.4.A.CHILD (1.800.422.4453 where Crisis Counselors are available 24/7, and next steps for safety and support will be outlined.

Please also visit: First Love Yourself Counseling, at www.FLYCounseling.com where the author is available for consultation, engaging lectures, and presentations for your school or organizations.